CONTENTS

LittleBrother BOOKS

Published 2022.

Little Brother Books Ltd, Ground Floor, 23 Southernhay East, Exeter, Devon EX1 1QL
books@littlebrotherbooks.co.uk | www.littlebrotherbooks.co.uk

Printed in China. Xuantan Temple Industrial Zone, Gulao Town, Heshan, Guangdong.

WELCOME TO ROBLOX

Step into a universe of possibilities with Roblox – the online gaming platform that lets players explore thousands of games and even make their own!

GAMING SYSTEMS

Roblox can be played on almost any gaming system, from PC and mobile to PlayStation, Xbox and Nintendo Switch consoles.

ROBUX

Most Roblox games and items are completely free, while for others players will need to purchase in-game currency known as Robux.

GAMES TO PLAY

There are all sorts of Roblox games to play, including RPG, tycoon, sport, adventure, first-person shooters, simulator and many more.

PLAY WITH FRIENDS

It's possible to play games solo or team up with friends online for more fun. Find out more about online safety on page 78.

ROBLOX STUDIO

If you want to take things to the next level, then be sure to check out Roblox Studio and try making your very own video games!

Studio

Make Anything You Can Imagine
With our FREE and immersive creation engine

Start Creating

Make Anything   Reach Millions of Players

BIGGEST YOUTUBERS

For Roblox hints, tips and advice, be sure to check out some of the biggest YouTubers. Find out the top five most popular on page 74.

ROBLOX EVENTS

There's always something happening in the Roblox universe, such as live events, crossovers with big brands and special virtual worlds.

Spotify
island
ON
ROBLOX

MILLIONS OF GAMES

With over 40 million games to try and more than 43 million daily active players, Roblox is one of the biggest expanding online platforms in the world!

ROBLOX

GETTING STARTED

If it's your first time playing Roblox, here's what you need to get set up and started. You'll be a full-on gaming pro in no time at all!

HOW TO PLAY ROBLOX

To play Roblox, you'll need to have access to a computer, mobile device or video game console such as a PlayStation, Xbox or Nintendo Switch.

GETTING ONLINE

You'll also need to have access to an internet connection for online play. Be sure to check with whoever pays the broadband bill before you start playing.

CREATE AN ACCOUNT

Next, download the Roblox app or visit the site's homepage. From here you'll need to create an account and make sure a parent or guardian gives permission.

ROBLOX

SIGN UP AND START HAVING FUN!

Birthday

Month   Day   Year

Username

Password

Gender (optional)

Sign Up

ROBLOX ON YOUR DEVICE

App Store   Google Play   amazon appstore   XBOX ONE   Microsoft

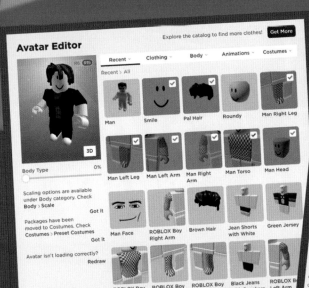

CREATE YOUR AVATAR

Once signed in, players will need to decide on the look and style of their virtual character, otherwise known as an avatar (see page 8).

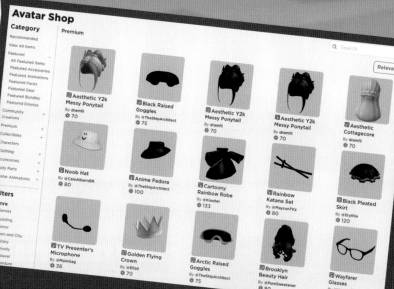

THE AVATAR SHOP

Players are able to buy Robux for playing some games and for purchasing premium items from the Avatar Shop (see pages 12 and 14).

AVAILABLE GAMES

When you're ready to play, search through all of the available Roblox games that are available and selectable via different categories.

WAITING TO PLAY

Some games allow players to jump right into the action straight away, while for others players have to wait for a new game to start before joining in.

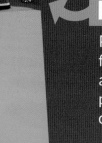

HOP IN!

Players can hop into a game for a short period, then leave and try a different title. Their progress will be saved, so they can continue at a later date.

CREATING AN AVATAR

One of the first things you'll need to do when beginning your Roblox journey is to create your own avatar. Let's find out how to get started!

HOW YOU APPEAR IN GAMES

Your avatar represents how you appear in most Roblox games. Take some time to think about what your character looks like before creating it.

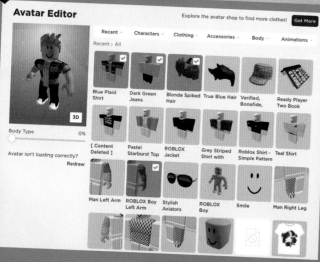

AVATAR EDITOR

The Avatar Editor section of the game lets players change everything about their character. From body type and shape, to height, weight and head size!

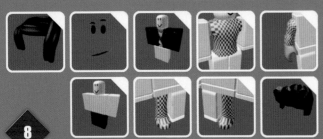

MIX AND MATCH

Once you've chosen the basics, move onto selecting your avatar's hair, face, clothing and accessories. Mix and match outfits to see what looks best.

THE AVATAR SHOP

Head on over to the Avatar Shop to start getting all sorts of clothes, character styles, animations, emotes, gear and other items.

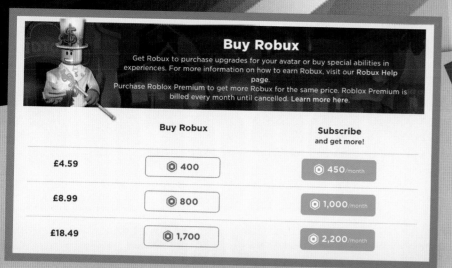

Buy Robux

Get Robux to purchase upgrades for your avatar or buy special abilities in experiences. For more information on how to earn Robux, visit our Robux Help page.
Purchase Roblox Premium to get more Robux for the same price. Roblox Premium is billed every month until cancelled. Learn more here.

	Buy Robux	Subscribe and get more!
£4.59	⬡ 400	⬡ 450/month
£8.99	⬡ 800	⬡ 1,000/month
£18.49	⬡ 1,700	⬡ 2,200/month

ROBUX

There are plenty of free items in the Avatar Shop, but to get others you'll have to spend Robux. Find out all about the in-game currency on pages 12-13.

WHAT WORKS BEST?

Once you have plenty of items, click on your profile and start playing around with the look of your avatar. Try on the items that you have to see what works best.

Recommended

Black Jeans	Ripped Skater Pants	Black Jeans with Sneakers	Black Jeans with White	Jean Shorts with White	I feel Bricky 2	Pink Jeans
By Roblox	By Roblox	By Roblox	By Roblox	By Roblox	By legodragon23	By Roblox
Free	Free	Free	Free	Free	Free	Free

Currently Wearing

You can take a look at your avatar in 2D or 3D to see how they will appear in-game from a variety of different angles.

2D

OTHER PLAYERS

Keep an eye out in your favourite games to see what other players are wearing. Some Roblox games even have their own special outfits that you can grab too!

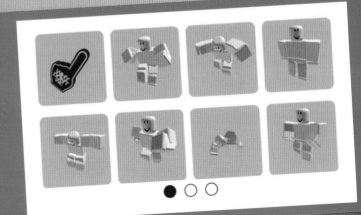

● ○ ○

GETTING STARTED

YOUR PROFILE PAGE

Once you've signed up for Roblox and created an avatar, you can keep track of your account on your very own player Profile page.

flateric1970
@flateric1970

1 Friends **5** Followers **0** Following

PROFILE PAGE

Your Profile page is the place to visit to find out more about your friends, followers, creations, avatar and much more.

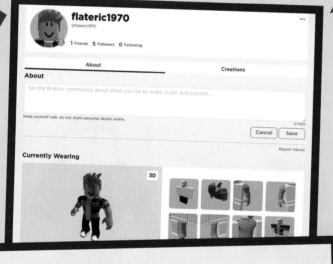

PROFILE PICTURE

Your Profile picture is a headshot of your avatar. If you change the look of your character, the picture on your account will change too.

ALL ABOUT

There's a section on your Profile page that allows you to tell the rest of the Roblox community all about yourself. Try writing something funny in there!

About

Roblox is my favourite ever video game! I get to hang out with my friends and find out what they're playing too. Check out my creations and send me a friend request if you want to team up!

My Inventory

CATEGORY	HATS
Animations	Showing 1 - 24 of 231 results
Audio	
Badges	
Decals	
Faces	
Game Passes	
Gear	
Hats	
Heads	
Models	
Packages	
Pants	
Faces	

Explore the catalog to find more hats! **Get More**

Casey's Shades
By: ROBLOX

Casey's Hair
By: ROBLOX

John's Scarf
By: ROBLOX

John's Hair
By: ROBLOX

Claire's Shades
By: ROBLOX

Claire's Hair
By: ROBLOX

Serena's Scarf
By: ROBLOX

Serena's Hair
By: ROBLOX

Lin's Glasses
By: ROBLOX

Lin's Hair
By: ROBLOX

Oakley's Glasses
By: ROBLOX

Oakley's Hair
By: ROBLOX

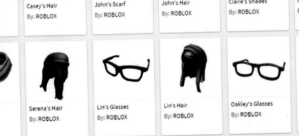

2016 ROBLOX Calend
By: ROBLOX

2016 New Years Glass
By: ROBLOX

Brown Furry Animal H
By: ROBLOX
100

Winged Helmet of Ach
By: ROBLOX

Portrait of a Hero in R
By: ROBLOX

Opened Hard Gift of A
By: ROBLOX

INVENTORY

Looking deeper into your Profile, you can also check out what items you have in your Inventory as part of your Collections (see pages 16-17).

BADGES

The Profile page shows what Roblox Badges you may have picked up since you started playing and any Badges earned from games.

Roblox Badges

Veteran

Badges

See All →

Net Worth - 10M

Net Worth - 1M

Net Worth - 10...

Net Worth - 10K

Welcome to M...

Welcome! 🐾

Experiences

flateric1970's Place

This is your very first Roblox creation. Check it out, then make it your own with Roblox Studio!

Active
0

Visits
0

CREATIONS

The Creations page of your profile always includes information on the very first place you made. You can also take a look at it later in Roblox Studio.

ROBLOX BLOG

The side menu next to your Profile page lets you send and receive messages from other gamers, trade (see pages 12-13), join groups and check out the Roblox blog.

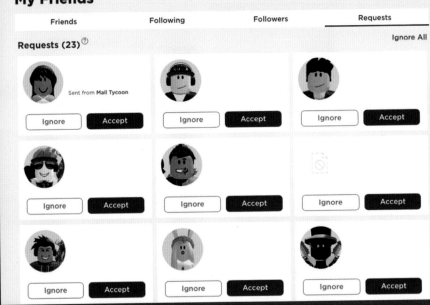

My Friends

| Friends | Following | Followers | Requests |

Requests (23) ⑦

Ignore All

Sent from Mall Tycoon

Ignore   Accept
Ignore   Accept
Ignore   Accept
Ignore   Accept
Ignore   Accept
Ignore   Accept
Ignore   Accept
Ignore   Accept
Ignore   Accept

FRIENDS

In the My Friends section, are requests from people you know and others you may have played with in games. Choose to accept or ignore any friends' requests.

ROBUX

There are plenty of free items for your avatar, but to get others you'll need to spend Robux. This is the Roblox in-game currency that can bought or earned.

SPENDING SPREE

Some of the best items in the Roblox Avatar Shop cost money. These can include clothing, accessories, game passes and in-game microtransactions.

BUYING ROBUX

Players can buy Robux in the game or via the Roblox website using real money. The value of Robux can range from 400, right up to 10,000!

GIFT CARDS

Many stores, such as Amazon, sell Roblox Gift Cards. These are available in various amounts and also include exclusive limited time virtual items.

ROBLOX PREMIUM

Players who really want to take their gaming to the next level can sign up to Roblox Premium. For a subscription fee users will be gifted Robux every month, as well as special items.

TRADING

Only Roblox Premium members are able to trade items in the game. Players can accept or decline offers for items, if they agree or disagree with the asking price.

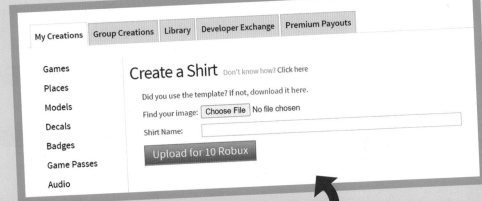

WATCH OUT FOR SCAMS

There are lots of links online that offer 'Free Robux' from people you don't know. These are most likely scams, so be sure not to click on them or send them any money.

TIME FOR TIX

When Roblox first launched it included two in-game currencies: Robux and Tix. However, Tix were eventually dropped altogether in 2016.

CLOTHING FEE

In 2021 Roblox rolled out a Clothing Fee, which required players to pay 50 Robux to upload a Shirt, Pants or T-shirt for sale. This was later lowered to just 10 Robux.

EARN ROBUX

It's possible to earn lots of Robux, by making and selling items to other players. Developers get paid in Robux, which they can then cash out for real-world money.

8 MILLION Developers

20 MILLION Experiences

30.6 BILLION Hours engaged since 2008*

$329 MILLION Dollars paid to the community developers*

SPEND WISELY

Some of the much rarer items in Roblox are very expensive, so you may want to think carefully before spending your hard-earned Robux on them!

Violet Valkyrie
By ROBLOX ✓ Item Owned

This item is available in your inventory.

Price	◉ 50,000
Type	Accessory | Hat
Sales	1,294
Genres	Medieval , Adventure
Description	Be joyful in victory.

GETTING STARTED

AVATAR SHOP

You can customise your avatar in all sorts of ways. Head to the Avatar Shop and pick up lots of different items to get started!

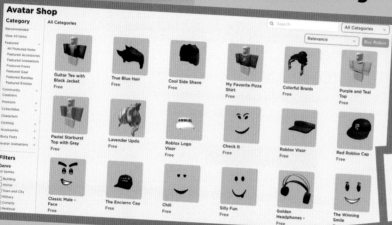

THE AVATAR SHOP

The Avatar Shop can be accessed from the main Roblox menu. Inside are a variety of items, all arranged in different categories for easy access.

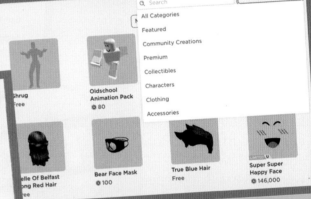

BROWSE ITEMS

Browse items by Featured, Community Creations, Premium, Collectibles, Characters, Clothing, Accessories, Body Parts and Animations.

DROPDOWN MENU

Once you've selected a category, it's also possible to select a dropdown menu that shows Most Favourited, Bestselling and Updated items.

FILTERS

Filters in the Shop allow you to see items from certain genres (such as Sci-Fi, Sports, RPGs), from Creators and even unavailable items.

Tuxedosam Backpack

By @Sanrio

Price	◎ 200	**Buy**

Type	Accessory | Back
Genres	All
Updated	Apr 23, 2022
Description	Try on this stylish Tuxedosam backpack! Have you ever seen a backpack with a tie?

Try On 3D

☆ 27K+

FIND OUT MORE

Items in the Avatar Shop are arranged in a grid pattern. Clicking on one of the items allows you to find out more about it and how much it costs.

Black Raised Goggles
By @TheShipArchitect
◎ 75

Black Pleated Skirt
By @Erythia
◎ 120

Shattered Minions
By @GuestCapone
◎ 125

Right Face Bandage
By @TheShipArchitect
◎ 100

Void Antlers
By @Urbanize
◎ 140

Helmet Goggles
By @JohnDrinkin
◎ 75

Aesthetic Y2k Messy Ponytail
By dramfii
◎ 70

Anime Fedora
By @TheShipArchitect

Blonde Farmgirl Beaut

Feathered War

PREMIUM

Many items in the Shop are free, but some are Premium and cost Robux to buy. The more currency you have the rarer the stuff you can get!

YOUR INVENTORY

Once you've bought an item, it appears in your Inventory. You can then place it on your avatar character to see how it will look in-game.

My Inventory

Explore the avatar shop to find more Accessories! **Get More**

Accessories > Head

Category

Accessories   >

Animations

Audio

Avatar Animations   >

Badges

Verified, Bonafide,
By **Roblox**
Offsale

Ready Player Two Book
By **Roblox**
Offsale

Category

Explore the avatar shop to find more Accessories!

Accessories > Head

Accessories   >

Animations

Audio

Avatar Animations   >

Badges

Bottoms   >

Bundles

Classic Clothing   >

International Fedora -
By **Roblox**
Free

Roblox Visor
By **Roblox**
Free

Golden Headphones -
By **Roblox**
Free

AOTP Hat - KSI
By **Roblox**
Free

< Page 1 >

OTHER'S INVENTORY

Be sure to check out other player's inventories to see what cool things they have. Some even sell or trade items for you to add to your collection.

BADGES and ACHIEVEMENTS

Show your friends how awesome you are at playing Roblox by collecting special badges and getting a full set of achievements!

ALL KINDS TO COLLECT

Once you start playing Roblox you'll be able to earn special badges. There are all kinds to collect including Gamer, Developer and Community categories.

Badges

Membership Badges

 Welcome To The Club Badge
This badge is awarded to users who have ever belonged to the illustrious Builders Club. These people are part of a long tradition of Roblox greatness.

Community Badges

 Administrator Badge
This badge identifies an account as belonging to a Roblox administrator. Only official Roblox administrators will possess this badge. If someone claims to be an admin, but does not have this badge, they are potentially trying to mislead you. If this happens, please report abuse and we will delete the imposter's account.

 Veteran Badge
This badge recognizes members who have visited Roblox for one year or more. They are stalwart community members who have stuck with us over countless releases, and have helped shape Roblox into the experience that it is today. These medalists are the true steel, the core of the Robloxian history ... and its future.

 Friendship Badge
This badge is given to members who have embraced the Roblox community and have made at least 20 friends. People who have this badge are good people to know and can probably help you out if you are having trouble.

 Ambassador Badge
This badge was awarded during the Am... retired and is no longer attainable.

PROFILE PAGE

Every badge you earn can be viewed on your Profile page. Selecting Badges lets you see which ones you have and what they're for.

Hair
Heads
Meshes
Models
Passes
Places
Plugins
Private Servers
Shoes
Tops
Video

 Welcome to Bakery
By Babble Games
Offsale

 Get going
By The Gang Sto...
Offsale

Welcome
By The Gang Sto...
Offsale

Survived a Disaster
By @Stickmasterl...
Offsale

Stage 10
By @Bloxtun
Offsale

Survivor
By @Polyhex
Offsale

 Supercharge...
By @Polyhex
Offsale

It's A Blast!
By @Polyhex
Offsale

4 Floors Complete
By Grandma's Fa...
Offsale

Junior Programmer
By @ady1111
Offsale

 Graduate
By @ady1111
Offsale

 Student
By @ady1111
Offsale

 Learner
By @ady1111
Offsale

 Thanks for playing
By @ady1111
Offsale

 Welcome to Dino Park!
By Vanity Studio
Offsale

Roblox Badges

 Administrator
 Friendship
Combat Initiation
Homestead
Bricksmith
 Inviter
Outrageous Builder...
Warrior
Welcome To The Cl...

Roblox Badges

 Administrator
 Friendship
Combat Initiation
Homestead
Bricksmith
 Inviter
Outrageous Builder...
Warrior
Welcome To The Cl...

EARNING BADGES

Some badges can be earned just by playing games, changing the look of your avatar, joining your friends online or having awesome creations.

Welcome to Mega Mansion Tycoon!

By Wild Atelier ⬤ Item Owned

Type	Badge
Updated	Mar 04, 2022
Description	Welcome to town! You've played Mega M... Tycoon

EASY TO GET HOLD OF

Some badges are easy to get hold of and some are very rare. Some are listed as 'Impossible', with only a 0.9% chance of players getting them!

Creating Badges

You should have an image ready for the badge's icon in either `.jpg`, `.gif`, `.png`, `.tga`, or `.bmp` format. When you're creating the image, use a template of **512×512 pixels**.

As the upload process will trim and crop the final badge into a circular image, don't include important details outside of the circular boundaries.

Note that you can create up to 5 badges for free in a 24-hour period (GMT) for each experie... you want to create more badges within the 24-hour period, it costs **100 Robux** per additio...

To create a badge:

1. In the **Home** tab of the menu bar, navigate to the **Settings** section and click **Game** **Game Settings** menu displays.
2. In the left-hand navigation, select **Monetization**.

CREATING BADGES

Official badges are created by Roblox, but it's also possible for players to make their own. These have to be created in Roblox Studio then added to the game.

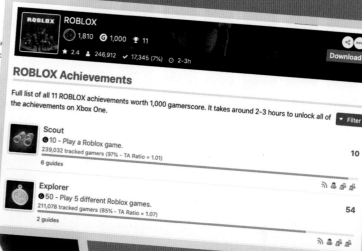

ACHIEVEMENTS

As well as badges, players can impress their mates with achievements. There are 11 official Roblox achievements to get, which can all be done in a single day!

PLAY WITH FRIENDS

Achievements include playing 15 Roblox games, taking part in a game with three of your friends, rating five games and many others.

PLAYER BADGES

Completing all 11 official Roblox achievements gets you a cool Player Badge icon added to your collection and gamer points on PCs and Xbox consoles.

RPG

Games in Roblox fall into different categories or types. From the home page you can see what experiences are available to play.

Role-Playing Games (or RPG) are some of the most popular titles available. Most involve players taking part in epic fantasy quests!

Some games are also known as MMORPG or Massively Multiplayer Online Role-Playing Game, with players joining teams or parties, working together.

There are lots of awesome RPG titles that are free to play. These include Dungeon Quest, World // Zero, Swordburst 2, RPG World and Vesteria.

In RPGs players have to explore strange worlds, battle enemies, level up and find new items to become even stronger characters.

TOWN AND CITY

Some of the best Roblox games are open-world or building-focused. These usually take place in towns and city environments.

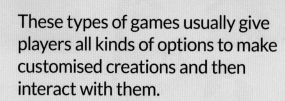

These types of games usually give players all kinds of options to make customised creations and then interact with them.

Some of the best town and city games available include Mad City, Welcome to Bloxburg, MeepCity, Welcome to Farmtown!, RoCitizens and more.

Many town and city games can be endless experiences. Even if you do manage to complete them, you can then build something new and start again!

19

BUILDING

Lots of Roblox players love to build and make things. The good news is that there are all sorts of awesome building games to play.

From wide-open sandbox games and PvP building challenges to survival and house-decorating titles, there's something for everyone.

If you want to check out some of the most fun Roblox building games just try Adopt Me!, Islands, Obby Creator, Whatever Floats Your Boat and RoVille.

Players who are looking to take their building talents to the next level can also sign up to Roblox Studios and make their own games!

TYCOON

If you've ever wanted to try your hand at running your own business and making money, then tycoon games are definitely for you!

When starting a new tycoon game, players have limited funds and have to start with basic items before they can earn money to buy better stuff.

In no time at all you'll be earning millions and spending that cash on even more expensive items. Spend plenty to get all of the best things.

When it comes to great tycoon games, check out Hospital Tycoon, Clone Tycoon 2, Tropical Resort Tycoon, Mega Mansion Tycoon and Mall Tycoon.

21

SPORT

For players who like to give their fingers a real workout, there are plenty of fast-paced sports titles to get to grips with!

Whether it's football, basketball, dodgeball or golf, there's probably a Roblox experience that exists for fans of almost any sport.

There are all kinds of top sports titles to try, such as Roblox Dodgeball!, Kick Off, Sports City, Phenom and Super Striker League.

Most Roblox sports games can be played solo but are much more fun when you team up with friends for some one-on-one action!

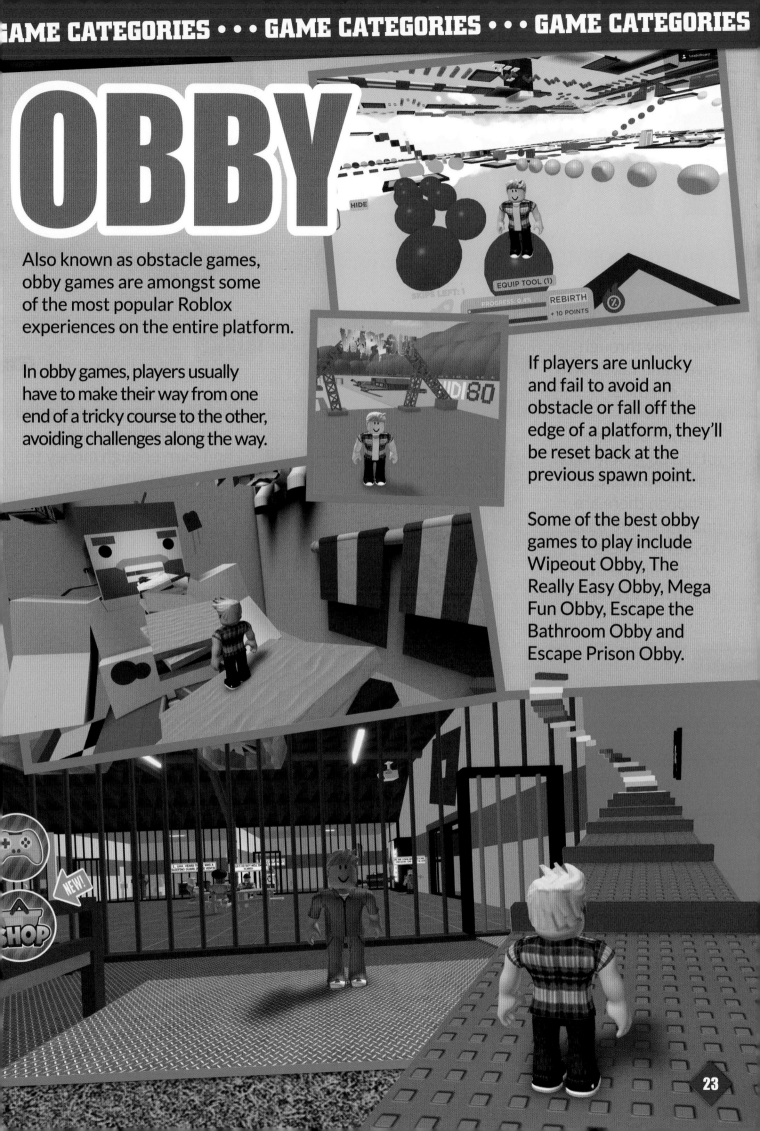

OBBY

Also known as obstacle games, obby games are amongst some of the most popular Roblox experiences on the entire platform.

In obby games, players usually have to make their way from one end of a tricky course to the other, avoiding challenges along the way.

If players are unlucky and fail to avoid an obstacle or fall off the edge of a platform, they'll be reset back at the previous spawn point.

Some of the best obby games to play include Wipeout Obby, The Really Easy Obby, Mega Fun Obby, Escape the Bathroom Obby and Escape Prison Obby.

FPS

Also known as First Person Shooters, these Roblox games allow players to blast their way through levels and take down their enemies.

FPS title are some of the biggest Roblox games available, although there are many that are basic copies of others so may not be that much fun to play.

In FPS, players have to grind away in order to level up and earn enough money to purchase better weapons, abilities and upgrades.

If you want to try out some of the best FPS games go for Zombie Uprising, Energy Assault, Shoot Out!, Island Royale and BIG! Paintball.

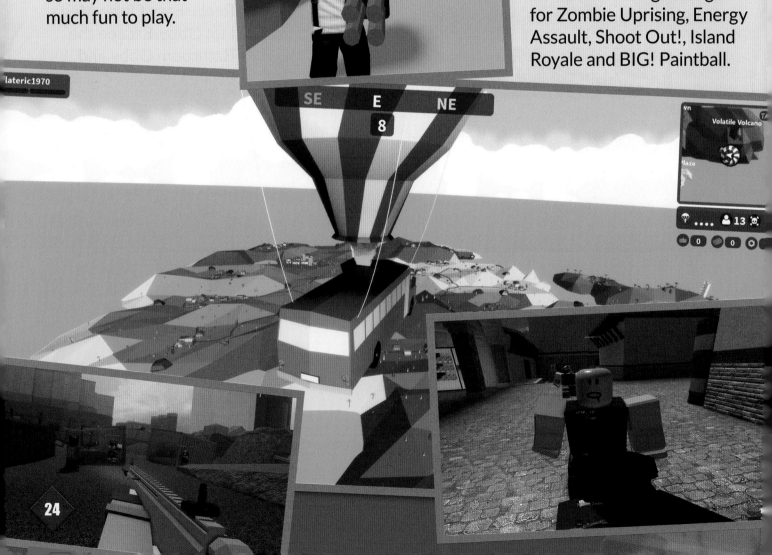

ADVENTURE

There are lots of adventure games to play in Roblox including platformers, open-world exploration titles and even hide and seek!

With thousands of Roblox adventure games to choose from, it can often be a little tricky to work out which ones are the best.

Before you start adventuring, think about the sort of games you like playing, how long you want to spend on them and if you want to play solo.

flateric1970

When it comes to the very best Roblox adventure games, try Robot 64, Little World, Hide and Seek Extreme, Shark Bite and Royale High.

Shark health

Choosing the next shark

STORE

THE SHARK HAS BEEN RELEASED

Chance To Be Shark

SIMULATOR

There are all kinds of awesome simulator Roblox games to play and some of them are completely crazy!

Simulators let players try lots of different things, from being a strongman and running a laundry to unboxing and being an animal.

In most simulators, players start out at a very basic level and have to get plenty of practice in order to progress through the game.

If you're looking for brilliant simulators then play Strongman Simulator, Laundry Simulator, Animal Simulator, Unboxing Simulator and Bee Swarm Simulator.

FIGHTING

Do you have what it takes to become a fighting champion? If so, then try your hand at the awesome Roblox bruisers!

The Roblox game engine isn't the best when it comes to true fighting games, but there are still plenty of fun titles worth playing.

In some fighting games players just use their fists, but in others they'll have access to weapons and even amazing superpowers.

Have a trusty moose that will be there for you in times of need

Some of the best fighting games Roblox has to offer include Anime Fighters Simulator, Ninja Legends, Boss Fighting Simulator, Muscle Legends and Blox Fruits.

ROBLOX STUDIO

If you're looking for more than just being a player and want to make your own games, Roblox Studio is the place to be!

STUDIO LAUNCH

Roblox Studio was released on PC and MacOS platforms for free in 2005 and is aimed at both new and experienced game developers.

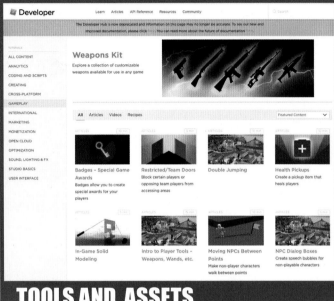

TOOLS AND ASSETS

In Roblox Studio, it's possible to create almost any kind of games you can think of using a variety of handy tools and assets.

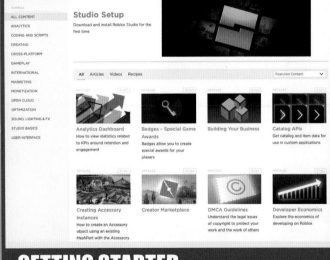

GETTING STARTED

To get started, users need to sign up for a Roblox account and download Roblox Studio to begin making awesome content.

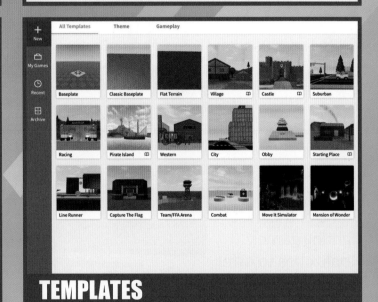

TEMPLATES

There are all sorts of 3D templates, objects and models to use in Roblox Studio. They can all be changed and adapted to fit your games.

SELL TO OTHER PLAYERS

As well as games, Roblox Studio also allows players to create your very own unique items and game passes to sell on to others for Robux.

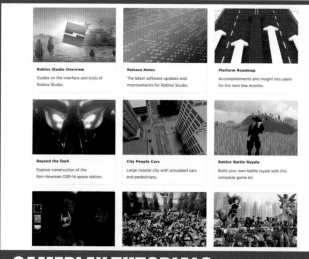

GAMEPLAY TUTORIALS

To get up to speed quickly, you can check out the Roblox Studio gameplay tutorials and even dive into the coding and scripts pages.

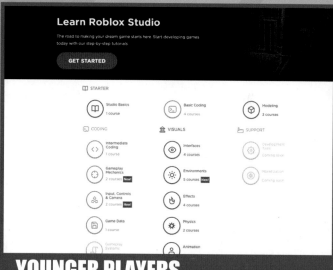

YOUNGER PLAYERS

Because Roblox Studio is easy to get to grips with, even many younger players have been able to use it to make their own games.

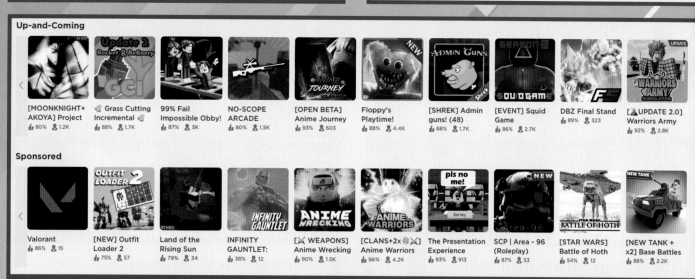

GAMES

Over 20 million games are created each year using Roblox Studio! Many of them are very basic though and are never added to the main game.

TOP 10

ROBLOX GLITCHES

With so many games available to play on Roblox, there are bound to be some that have a few bugs or glitches. How many of these mistakes have you seen?

#10

MULTI-JUMP

Often seen in the game Jailbreak, this bug allows PC players to jump higher than usual. Just add gears to your backpack and press the number key linked to it whilst holding the space bar.

#9

TRANSPARENCY TRICK

This was a glitch that used to occur in Roblox years ago. Putting a certain texture on older solid bodies would make players transparent or like the object you were wearing.

#8

SWORD LUNGE FLY

This PC bug can be performed in Bridge Sword Fight. Whilst holding a sword, double-click and put it away to start floating off into the sky!

#1

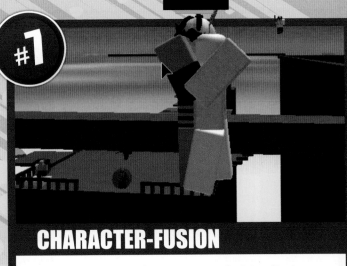

CHARACTER-FUSION

Although long since removed, this glitch allowed two players to face each other, turn the camera to face the direction they were going in and then fuse together.

#6 2009 PLAYER BADGE

Another blast from the past, this bug let players make as many badges as they wanted. In fact, it was possible to create infinite badges for just 100 Robux.

#5 SIDE-WALKING

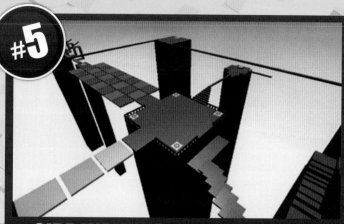

This simple glitch used to allow players to move around in the air without falling. It was possible to perform it in the Sword Fight on the Heights game.

#4 UNKNOWN USERNAME

Only ever seen when testing games in Roblox Studio, a player's username appears as 'Unknown' and their avatar is just a plain dummy character. That's just weird!

#3 UNATTACHED HEAD

An extremely rare glitch where an avatar spawns and then its head falls off onto the ground! You'll still be able to play as normal, but your head stays where it is.

#2 INVISIBLE ACCESSORIES

Back in July and August 2021, a number of accessories in the Avatar Shop would be invisible. They included Dart Glasses, Mech Wings, Snow Friend and Pumpkin Patch.

#1 MAGICAL UNICORN

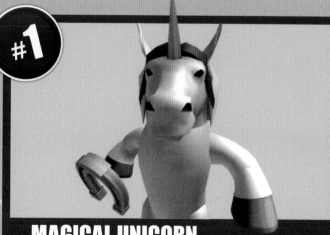

Try equipping the Magical Unicorn in Roblox High School and then driving a vehicle. Some of them will go completely haywire whilst you're sat in them!

5 DUNGEON QUEST ■ ■ ■ ■ ■

Featuring an amazing art style and a combination of RPG and dungeon-crawling elements, this RPG is packed with amazing features.

There are plenty of unique enemies to battle and lots of items to find along the way. Level up to unlock more abilities, weapons and armour.

Dungeon Quest has recently been updated and now features loot, daily rewards and new bosses from the frozen Northern Lands!

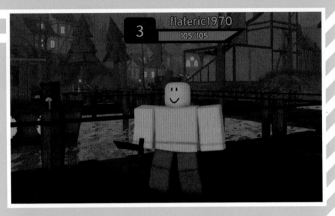

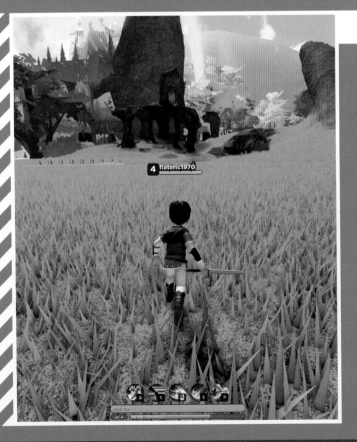

4 WORLD // ZERO ■ ■ ■ ■

Easily one of the best Roblox RPGs available, World // Zero was created in 2019 and is a truly epic RPG enjoyed by millions of fans.

The game has an anime art style, fun combat mechanics and a good selection of character classes to choose from.

There are all sorts of tough enemies to battle alone or in a party, including dragons, demons and dungeon bosses guarding loot.

3 SWORDBURST 2

With a truly vast world to explore, Swordburst 2 offers players plenty of up-close combat with a range of challenging foes.

Players will need to put in some time grinding in order to get hold of the best loot and gear, but the effort is definitely worth it.

Defeating bosses will allow players to unlock new areas of the world to explore and even rarer items to find.

2 RPG WORLD

A classic Roblox game, RPG World was released in 2019 and has since had over 50 million visits from players.

There are usually hundreds of players online at any given time, meaning there's always someone to team up with.

Defeat monsters, level up and get better gear. With regular updates, codes for free Crystals and more, RPG World has it all.

VESTERIA

Not only one of the most popular RPGs, but also one of the best Roblox games, Vesteria is the ultimate MMORPG.

Originally a pay-to-play title, Vesteria is now free, allowing players to band together and battle the world's many enemies.

Starting off on your own gives players the chance to learn all about the game's mechanics, how to earn money and level up.

As well as battling enemies and undertaking quests, it's also possible to farm for items and then either keep or sell them.

There are three weapons classes in Vesteria: Warrior, Mage and Hunter. Each allows players to figure out which ones they like best.

Characters can be customised with different looks, weapons and armour, depending on how much money you have.

Reaching Level 30 allows players to unlock three sub-classes for each class, allowing for even more customisation.

Bosses can be quite tough to face on your own, so you're better off joining a party with others to take them down.

5 MAD CITY

Take to the streets of Mad City as either a crimefighting superhero or a villain out to cause as much chaos as possible!

Nearly 2 billion players have visited Mad City and it's easy to see why. The game is open-world and there's always something to do.

Help the police stop criminals, prevent a bank heist, escape from prison or battle your enemies – it's completely up to you!

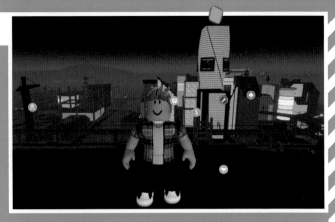

4 WELCOME TO BLOXBURG

One of the most popular Roblox games of all times, Welcome to Bloxburg has been visited over 5 billion times to date.

Choose a character, customise them and your house, then head out into the city to take part in activities or get a job.

The game may look simple but there's always plenty to see and do, as well as lots of other players to interact with.

3 MEEPCITY ■ ■ ■ ■ ■ ■ ■

With some RPG and customisation elements, MeepCity is a huge town and city game that has gigantic servers and lots of players.

Players can edit their characters and homes, earn coins to buy more items, play games and chat with others online.

With a whole city to explore, you'll never be short of something fun to take part in or challenging tasks to complete.

2 WELCOME TO FARMTOWN! ■ ■

Get ready to start farming, mining, ranching, cooking and exploring in one of the most popular Roblox games.

The first Roblox title to feature global chat, Welcome to Farmtown! also allows players to raise animals, visit fairgrounds and much more.

Explore outside the local town and you might just find rare fossils, or you can try your hand at growing strange alien fruit!

ROCITIZENS

There really is no better town and city game in Roblox than RoCitizens. Released in 2013, it's also one of the oldest on the platform.

Players get to live in a sprawling city where they can work at a job, complete quests, customize their homes and meet other players.

RoCitizens has grown a lot in recent years, with regular updates adding new features, locations and items to discover.

Unlike other town and city games, RoCitizens also includes destructible environments and boasts a massive open-world.

A recent update to the game has added new neighbourhood locations to the city, with Beach and Mountain areas to explore.

Having a job in the game allows players to earn money and then use their cash to buy new items for their homes.

Pop into the local café to meet up with other players and grab a drink or work there to boost your funds.

Check out the official RoCitizens store to pick up game passes for double wages, custom furniture, a speed boost and more.

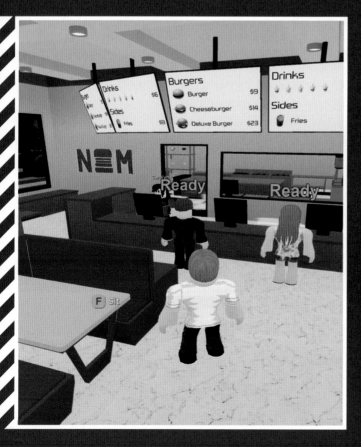

5 ADOPT ME!

As well as offering players the chance to hatch and care for a variety of cute pets, Adopt Me! also has plenty of building options.

When starting a game, players each get their own house which they can then customise with furniture, paint and other items.

Those things cost money though, so you'll need to earn cash by working and taking on various jobs within the game.

4 ISLANDS

A sandbox game inspired by Minecraft, Islands is very popular and offers the players the chance to build all kinds of things.

You begin the game on a small floating island in the sky and have to use basic tools and resources to get started.

Travel to other islands to collect more items with which to expand your base, fish, farm, raise animals and battle monsters.

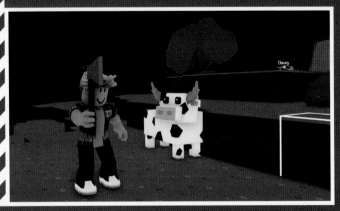

If you're looking for all sorts of great
construction games, then Roblox has you covered.
Here are the top five to check out.

3 OBBY CREATOR ■ ■ ■ ■ ■ ■ ■

For those of you who like playing obby games, here's your chance to make your own! This title has had over 200 million visits so far.

Obby Creator lets players build their own courses and see just how challenging they can make them for others to try out.

There are all sorts of tools and items to use, with some costing money. Players can also work together in the handy Team Build mode.

2 WHATEVER FLOATS YOUR BOAT ■

This is a slightly different kind of construction game, but it's one that's also fast-paced and loads of fun!

Players begin by building their own boats with blocks and weapons, then take to the sea to battle it out against each other.

The only way to win is to take out your opponents but watch out for players attacking you and your boat filling up with water.

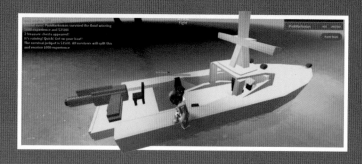

ROVILLE

With a massive open-world to explore and all sorts of building options, RoVille leads the way in Roblox construction games.

Players start off buying a ready-made house or instead they can choose to build their own home from the ground up.

Add walls, doors and windows to your house and even multiple floors to make it look exactly the way you want it to.

Although some of the buildings may look a bit odd, the sky's the limited when it comes to making anything that you like.

As well as construction, players can also take part in town and city-style activities and events to earn money for items and new builds.

Another way to get lots of cash is to take on a job for a salary or even go all-out and start your own booming business!

With the town being so large, the best way to get around is to buy yourself a vehicle, such as a cool sports car.

If you put your hard-earned money into a bank, you'll be able to save up and buy yourself a massive millionaire's mansion to customise.

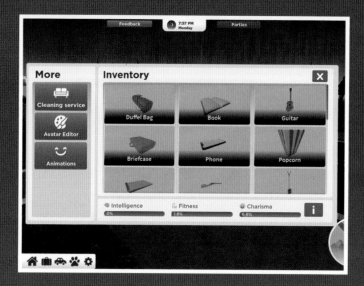

5 HOSPITAL TYCOON

If you've ever wanted to find out what making and running a busy Hospital would be like, then this is the Roblox experience for you.

Players can build their very own hospital, keep it running every day and earn money by looking after patients and upgrading everything.

A recent update even allows players to treat pets and hire new animal care staff, such as a vet. Use the code 'Pet' to get a free double cash bonus too.

4 CLONE TYCOON 2

What could be more fun than creating a clone army of yourself? That's exactly what you get to do in this game and so much more.

Send your clones in to battle to beat enemies and earn cash. You can then use that money to build better bases, weapons and items.

Levelling up gives players access to more fun stuff, such as a research lab to build better clones. Be sure to check out the new ice planet too!

When it comes to Tycoon games in Roblox, you're spoilt for choice. Try your hand at everything from running a hospital to owning an expensive mansion!

3 TROPICAL RESORT TYCOON ■ ■ ■

Head off on holiday for some sun, sea and surf in this fun Roblox experience. Build your very own tropical resort, complete with pool, rooms and vehicles.

Owning an island is as amazing as it sounds and you can explore the ocean, fly in a plane, check out obby courses and much more.

The happier your guests are, the more money you'll earn. This lets you upgrade your resort to make it even better and attract more visitors.

2 MEGA MANSION TYCOON ■ ■ ■

If showing off how much cash you have is your thing, then Mega Mansion Tycoon is the Roblox experience for you.

Those who've always wanted to be mega-rich can build their own amazing mansions and add on all sorts of luxuries, from a pool to fast cars.

Recent updates have added the ability for players to buy a boat dock, complete with jet ski, speedboat and other water-based craft.

MALL TYCOON ■ ■ ■ ■ ■ ■ ■

Shopping at the mall might be fun, but what if you could actually run the place? Well now you can thanks to Mall Tycoon!

In this game players get to build and run their own mall, earning money by adding extra stores, decorations and facilities.

If you add and expand the right areas, you'll attract more shoppers and then make even more money to buy better stuff.

Keeping shoppers happy is essential. If the face icon on screen is smiling, you'll know you're doing well and can earn big cash tips.

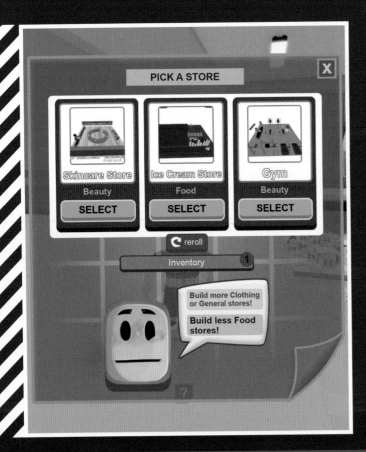

It's possible to add multiple levels to your mall, as well as a car park at the front, lifts, escalators, lighting, plants and more.

There are over 35 different stores that can be opened in your mall, from hairdressers and sports shops to restaurants and a cinema.

If you have any spare Robux you can spend them on useful items, including a handy Segway to speed around the mall.

Finish all 12 floors on your mall then head to the roof for a gold trophy, $1 million and a button to blow the whole thing up and start again from scratch!

5 ROBLOX DODGEBALL!

A popular sports title, Roblox Dodgeball! let's players hit the court and each other in a fast-paced game.

Matches feature 6 vs 6 action, as players try to hit as many of the opposing team with the ball as they can.

If you get hit four times, you're out of the game. One player is also the Juggernaut and has tons of health and is tougher to beat!

Intermission: 4

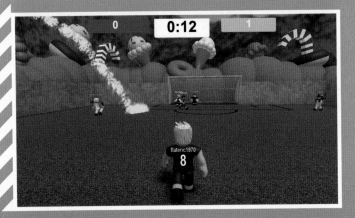

4 KICK OFF

A massively-successful football game, Kick Off has millions of fans who play all of the time to improve their skills.

Unlike other football titles, this game is played and watched from above, which can sometimes make it a bit tricky.

Selecting VIP servers allows players to choose which team they want to be on, including many famous squads.

If you're active and like player sports in real life, the good news is there are lots of Roblox games that are just as fun!

3 SPORTS CITY

Fans of all kinds of sports will want to check out this game as it includes basketball, volleyball, hockey and more.

In Sports City players wander around a large area, picking which games to try on their own or as part of a team.

New sports and activities are being added to the game all of the time, so keep checking back for new challenges.

2 PHENOM

Shoot hoops and become the best there is on the court in the fast-paced basketball game that is Phenom.

There are multiple modes to try, including training, tournament, playground, crossover and other options.

Players have to grind a bit to really unlock the best items in the game, but it's well worth it to become a champion.

WELCOME TO THE PHENOM PRACTICE FACIL

1

SUPER STRIKER LEAGUE ◼ ◼ ◼ ◼

Easily the best Roblox football game there is, Super Striker League is perfect for any fan of the world's most popular sport.

Join a squad with four other players and take on other teams to see how many goals you can score to win trophies for your club.

As well as all the usual football moves, players also have access to various special powers and abilities.

Progress through Super Striker League to unlock more items, upgrades and special powers to give yourself an edge over others.

Ranked mode lets Level 25+ players take on opponents with similar abilities for a true challenge of their skills.

Special events often occur during matches that can help or hinder a player's progress throughout the game.

Don't be surprised to see a ninja firing arrows at you or mummies rising from the dead to stop players in the middle of a match!

Super Striker League takes football to extremes with a Roblox sporting experience that really is like no other out there.

5 WIPEOUT OBBY

Released in 2015, Wipeout Obby is one of the earliest of these type of games to be made available on the Roblox platform.

Based on the famous television game show of the same name, players have to make their way from one end of a tricky course to the other.

There are lots of challenging obstacles to avoid along the way and you'll definitely end up falling in the water many, many times!

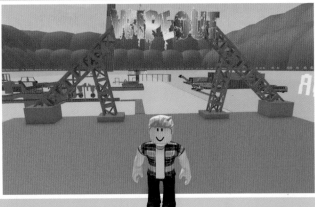

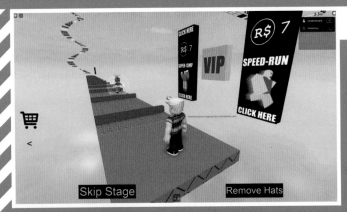

4 THE REALLY EASY OBBY

Don't believe the name of this game at all, as it is actually really challenging. You'll need plenty of skill to beat The Really Easy Obby.

Everything might look simple and colourful, but this is one Roblox title that will push each player's abilities to the limit.

Jump onto platforms, leap to floating pads, hop to conveyor belts and make it to safety as fast as you can to survive.

Obby games are some of the most fun
and challenging Roblox titles available.
Get ready to leap, hop and fall... a lot!

3 MEGA FUN OBBY

If you're looking for an obby game with lots of different courses to try, then Mega Fun Obby is definitely the one for you.

This game has the longest and largest collection of stages in any Roblox title, with over 2,650 levels to blast through.

Players can try their luck going through the levels on their own or against their friends to see who's the fastest.

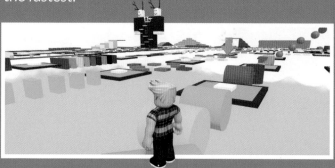

2 ESCAPE THE BATHROOM OBBY

This obby game is hilarious, mostly because it's packed with lots of funny obstacles to beat, all set in someone's bathroom!

Players have to make their way across objects such as giant toilet rolls, a bathtub, sink and more to reach the finish line.

That's not to say Escape the Bathroom Obby isn't a challenge though. It'll take real skill to make it to the end in one piece.

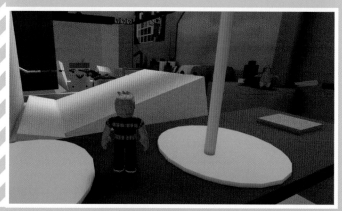

ESCAPE PRISON OBBY ■ ■ ■ ■ ■

Breaking out of a high-security prison gets even tougher in one of the most popular obby games available on Roblox.

When your character has been handed a 150-year jail sentence, they'll find themselves locked up in Robloxia's toughest prison.

Escape Prison Obby begins with players behind the bars of their cells. They'll need to find a way out and fast!

From this point on, things start to get a little crazy. There are all sorts of obstacles and challenges to avoid in each level.

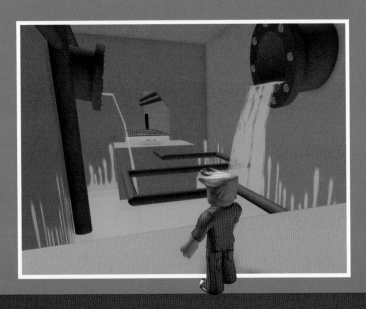

Players have to avoid guards, dogs, security systems, toxic waste and all sorts of other hazards to make it to freedom.

In some ways, Escape Prison Obby is a lot like the popular Floor is Lava games, but with other tricky elements thrown in.

Each level has a good balance of obstacles to beat and it's fun to see if you can do better than other players.

Escape Prison Obby has also been updated recently, with new levels and other features added, so be sure to check it out!

5 ZOMBIE UPRISING

Battle your way through wave after wave of the undead and try to stay alive in the fast-paced Zombie Uprising.

Players can try to make through each tough level on their own or team up in a squad of four players to survive.

To beat powerful boss enemies, you'll need to upgrade your weapons which can be selected from an impressive arsenal.

4 ENERGY ASSAULT

Set in a futuristic city, Energy Assault drops you straight into the action with a first-person shooter that never lets up.

As the title suggest, players can use a variety of energy-based weapons to take out their enemies in a series of maps.

There are different game modes to try, skins and outfits to unlock, daily missions to complete and much more.

When it comes to pulse-pounding first-person shooters, Roblox has you covered. Get ready to blast your way to victory!

3 SHOOT OUT! ■ ■ ■ ■ ■ ■ ■ ■

There's always something new to see in this first-person shooter, with regular updates and content being added all the time.

Shoot Out! has recently had a Heroes & Villains makeover, with appearances from lots of very-familiar characters.

The game has lots of really fun maps to play on, different skins and weapons, plus exclusive bonus rewards to the best players.

ONE SHOT MODE: FIRST TO 21 KILLS

2 ISLAND ROYALE ■ ■

You might recognise a lot of the elements in this FPS as Island Royale is an almost identical clone of the massive game, Fortnite.

Players are dropped onto an island level and have to survive by taking out their enemies with a variety of weapons.

Use your building skills to make elaborate structures from which to take cover and give yourself a tactical advantage.

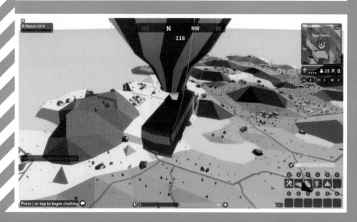

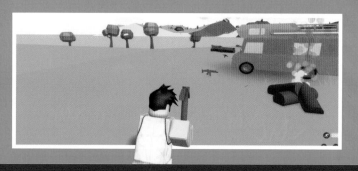

BIG PAINTBALL!

Unlike other grim and gritty FPS games, BIG Paintball! is all about having fun and getting completely splatted.

As in the real sport, players enter an arena as part of a team and have to work together to take out the opposing side.

Instead of lethal weapons, all players are armed with paintball guns that blast out a variety of different coloured pellets.

Each time you manage to hit a player, they'll be returned to the main spawn point in the level and re-join the action.

Players have to battle it out against the clock to try and score as many points as possible before the timer runs out.

It's possible to turn the entire battlefield into a complete mess by coating all walls, floors and ceilings with paintballs!

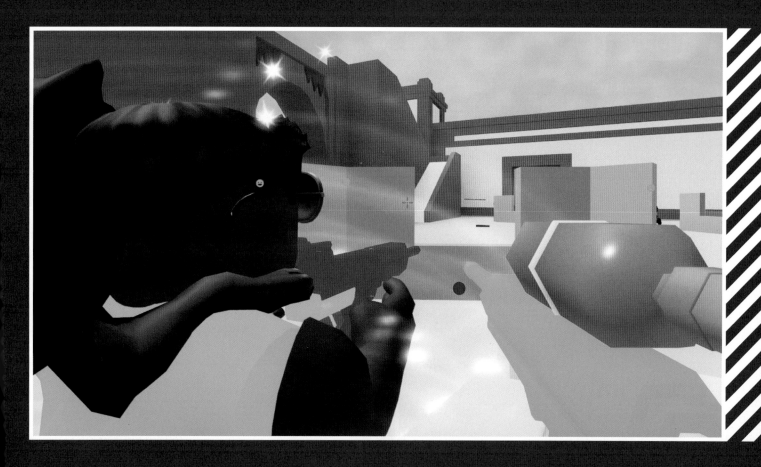

There's a good selection of weapons to choose from in the game, from pistols and automatics to cannons and sniper rifles.

Over 1.1 billion gamers have tried their hand at BIG Paintball! to date, which makes it a massive Roblox smash hit.

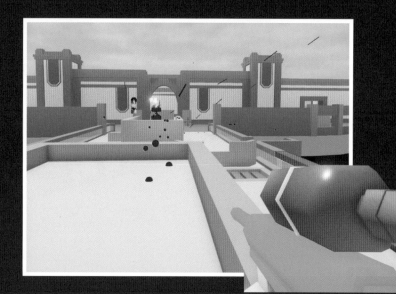

TOP 5

ADVENTURE

5 ROBOT 64

Taking inspiration from Mario 64, this fun game features a cute robot who has to help his master destroy the sun with ice cream.

Players take control of Beebo and have to guide the character around large stages, running, jumping and flying.

There are multiple enemies to fight and epic boss battles. This awesome 3D platforming adventure game has it all!

Dr. Smar

Your name is Beebo. Hear that? B-e-e-b-o. Me Smar, you Beebo.

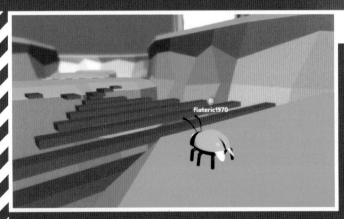

4 LITTLE WORLD

In Little World players take on the role of a tiny ladybug that has to survive in an overgrown garden and become bigger.

Unfortunately, there are lots of other creatures out there to get you, so you'll need to use all of your skills to survive.

Those that do reach the top of the food chain can then try to take on other players in the global leaderboards.

3 HIDE AND SEEK EXTREME ■ ■ ■

There are plenty of poor clones of this game, so be sure to check out the original for the best overall experience.

When the game starts, one player becomes the seeker and all others have to dash off and find a good hiding spot.

The seeker than has to find all of the other players before the timer resets and someone else takes on that role!

2 SHARKBITE ■ ■ ■ ■ ■ ■

In SharkBite, players get to become either the ravenous eating machine or a group of humans on a boat.

Players who are the shark have to swim around stealthily, attacking and destroying boats within a set time limit.

However, humans are armed with all sorts of weapons and it's their job to destroy the shark. This is one Roblox game with real bite!

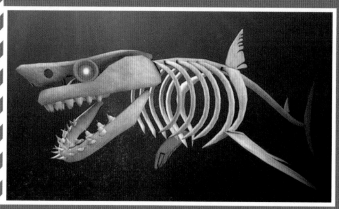

ROYALE HIGH ■ ■ ■ ■ ■ ■ ■

When it comes to hugely-successful Roblox games, Royale High stands out with over 7 billion visits since launch.

Players enter a unique fantasy world that's filled with lots of people to meet, magical lands to explore and fun games to play.

Royale High has a very loyal fanbase, with many players having stuck with the game since it launched back in 2017.

When starting the game, players can choose what they want their character to look like and then customise them.

It's possible to level up your character by attending classes at Royale High School. Better grades mean more rewards!

Players can earn Diamonds in the game and use the valuable currency to buy new items, boost skills and level up.

Travel across the many lands is easy thanks to the ability to teleport. Players need to explore everywhere to discover secrets.

Royale High is an awesome way to spend lots of time online with other players in an ever-growing dream world!

5 LAUNDRY SIMULATOR ∎ ∎ ∎

Who knew that running your own laundry could be this much fun? Get yourself in a spin with this awesome simulator!

Players have to compete against each other as employees to see who can wash and clean as many clothes as possible.

Your washing machine will eventually get so massive, it'll be possible to actually throw your friends inside and watch them spin.

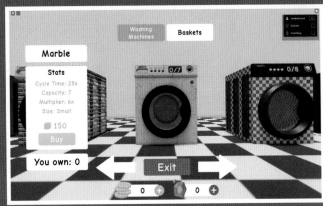

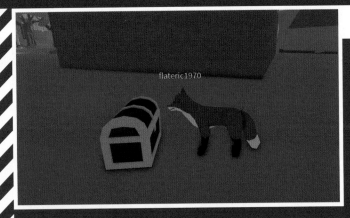

4 ANIMAL SIMULATOR ∎ ∎ ∎

In this game players can choose to be an animal or stay in human form and work together with their furry friends.

Experience what life could be like as an animal, choosing from a huge variety of real or special mystical creatures.

Play Animal Simulator solo or team up with others to beat bosses, collect treasure chests or even chat to each other.

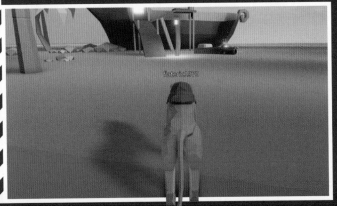

More and more simulation games are being added to Roblox all of the time, so there really is something for everyone.

3 UNBOXING SIMULATOR ■ ■ ■ ■

There's something really fun about boxing stuff and that's exactly what you'll be able to do plenty of in this game.

Unboxing Simulator allows players to smash open boxes of all different shapes and sizes to grab various goodies inside.

The game has loads of cool collectible items to find, including rare pets that can help you on your unboxing adventure.

2 BEE SWARM SIMULATOR ■ ■ ■

One of the most popular Roblox simulation games available, Bee Swarm Simulator will have you hooked right away.

Grow your own swarm of bees, collect pollen and unlock upgrades. Start out with a single bee and watch them multiply!

The more you play, the more money you'll earn. Use your cash to buy upgrades, boosts for your bees and special beans.

SONIC SPEED SIMULATOR ■ ■ ■ ■ ■

The official Sonic the Hedgehog game on Roblox is a blast! Race through multiple levels with SEGA's spikey blue hero.

In Sonic Speed Simulator, players can race through multiple stages to reach the finish line, whilst taking out enemies.

The faster you can make Sonic, the more you'll level up. Unlock more worlds and collect cute Chaos along the way.

Completing levels and challenges will reward players with more selectable characters and skins to show off to friends.

All-new adventures are regularly being added to Sonic Speed Simulator all the time, with rewards exclusive to each.

The more likes the game gets, the more rewards are added. These have included a mystery bonus and secret character skins.

Pick up rings to get currency and then spend your loot in the shop for even more amazing items and outfits.

Race against other players to see who is the fastest and earn special rewards. Can you beat your opponents and be a speed master?

5 ANIME FIGHTERS SIMULATOR

Over 800 million players have entered the world of Anime Fighters Simulator since it launched in 2021.

Explore islands, collect and train the strongest fighters and take on all enemies in some truly awesome combat.

There are also huge raids to take part in and earn shards, plus game passes, secret fighters, free items and much more.

4 NINJA LEGENDS

Learn how to become a stealthy warrior and take down a series of tough foes in the action epic, Ninja Legends.

Players need to make their way through a series of challenging islands and battling to level up and earn new weapons and skills.

Earning gems allows players to buy new items and belts, plus there are even pets to collect that help you in fights.

In fighting games, players get to learn all sorts of cool moves and combos in order to beat opponents and become champions!

3 BOSS FIGHTING SIMULATOR ■ ■ ■

One of the best Roblox bruisers available, Boss Fighting Simulator takes to the next level with massive enemies to beat.

The boss characters in the game are huge and just keep getting bigger. Defeat them to level up and earn coins.

Spend your winnings to upgrade weapons and then take on other players in the game's challenging PvP mode.

2 MUSCLE LEGENDS ■ ■ ■ ■ ■

In this game, players have to first train at gyms to build up their strength and stamina before entering battles.

Players who manage to boost their skills enough can fight CPU opponents and also enter PvP scraps to become Muscle King.

Muscle Legends isn't all about fighting though. There's also a fun pet collecting system for when you're not in the ring.

BLOX FRUITS

One of the biggest (and best) Roblox fighting games, Blox Fruits has had over 5 billion visits since it arrived in 2019.

Players can battle it out with others to become a master swordsman and the strongest fighter who's ever lived.

Safe Zone - PvP disabled

Choose to be either a pirate or a seaman and see which group can work together to take down their enemies.

As well as tough foes to defeat, there are also even more challenging and powerful boss battles to survive.

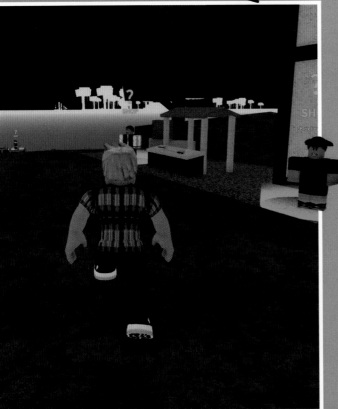

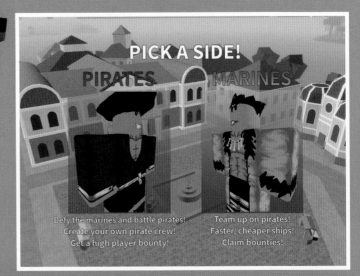

PICK A SIDE!

PIRATES   MARINES

Defy the marines and battle pirates!   Team up on pirates!
Create your own pirate crew!   Faster, cheaper ships!
Get a high player bounty!   Claim bounties!

Travel across the vast Blox Fruits world, encountering other characters and sailing across the ocean to find secrets.

New content is regularly being added to the game to keep players coming back, including islands, raids and weapons.

There are also plenty of different types of fruit to find. Collecting these gives players unique spells to use in combat.

Blox Fruits usually has an active player base of around 80,000, so there's always someone online to challenge!

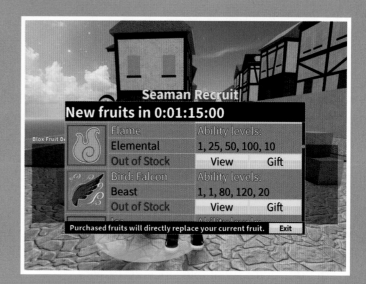

TOP 10 MOST EXPENSIVE ITEMS

Some items in Roblox are free, with others costing Robux. Then there are the rare premium items that are super-expensive!

#10 SPARKLE TIME BANDANAS

Available in red, green and blue the Sparkle Time Bandanas are available for 8,000 Robux each, which is around £77.

#9 HORNS OF THE CREATURE

Scare your enemies with this horned headdress. This was a limited time item but is now on sale for all for 8,000 Robux.

#8 MR. TENTACLES

Here's your chance to own a yellow squid of your own! Available since 2019, Mr. Tentacles will cost you 9,090 Robux.

#1 POOR MAN

You'd probably look this sad too if you'd spent 10,000 Robux (£100) on this very expensive face for your avatar.

#6

BLUESTEEL SWORDPACK

This epic back accessory also costs 10,000 Robux but is guaranteed to impress your friends and it looks cool in battles.

#5

GLORIOUS EAGLE WINGS

Soar through the air in style with the Glorious Eagle Wings. For just 10,000 Robux you too can own this awesome item.

#4

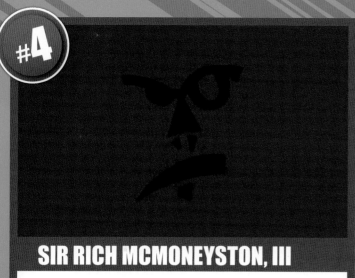

SIR RICH MCMONEYSTON, III

Show other Roblox players just how much cash you have to spend by buying this super-rich guy's face for 10,001 Robux.

#3

KORBLOX DEATHSPEAKER

Favourited more than 403,000 times, the fearsome Korblox Deathspeaker bundle will set you back 17,000 Robux (£165).

#2

SUMMER VALK

It may only be a hat accessory, but Summer Valk is very pricey. Anyone seen wearing it has spent 25,000 Robux (£243).

#1

VIOLET VALKYRIE

This hat accessory is the single most expensive item in Roblox. If you can afford it, it will cost a whopping 50,000 Robux (£486)!

TOP 10 ROBLOX YouTubers

If you're looking for the best Roblox YouTube channels to be watching, then these are the 10 biggest streamers to check out!

#10 DANTDM

One of the most successful YouTubers, DanTDM's channel has over 25 million subscribers. He posts videos about Roblox, Minecraft and Pokémon.

#9 TOFUU

Having started creating his own YouTube video in 2011, Tofuu' Roblox channel is essential viewing. Over 4 million other gamers think so too!

#8 FLAMINGO

With funny jokes, characters sketches and comedy clips, Flamingo posts some of the funniest Roblox videos you can find.

#1 DENIS

This Roblox YouTube channel was started in 2016, but now also includes videos about other popular video games such as Minecraft.

INQUISITORMASTER

Thanks to a massive following of over 9 million fans, InquisitorMaster is also one of Roblox's talented creators' list and it's easy to see why.

SKETCH

When it comes to big numbers. Sketch's YouTube channel is way ahead of the game. His Roblox videos have over 1.4 billion views to date.

THINKNOODLES

One of the most famous Roblox YouTubers, Thinknoodles started his channel in 2011. He has over 8 million subscribers and 3 billion video views.

GAMINGWITHKEV

Get ready to laugh your socks off when you check out GamingWithKev's hilarious Roblox videos. His channel also has over 8 million followers.

ITSFUNNEH

Although she only started posting Roblox videos in 2016, ItsFunneh's content is really funny and has led to gaining over 8 million subscribers.

ETHAN GAMER

British YouTuber Ethan Gamer is only 15 years old, but already has over 3 million subscribers thanks to his popular series of Roblox videos.

TOP 50 ROBLOX GAMES CHECKLIST

How many of the games in this Roblox Guide have you played? Give them all a go and track your progress by ticking each box!

RPGs

- [ ] Dungeon Quest
- [ ] World // Zero
- [ ] Swordburst 2
- [ ] RPG World
- [ ] Vesteria

TOWN AND CITY

- [ ] Mad City
- [ ] Welcome to Bloxburg
- [ ] MeepCity
- [ ] Welcome to Farmtown!
- [ ] RoCitizens

BUILDING

- [ ] Adopt Me!
- [ ] Islands
- [ ] Obby Creator
- [ ] Whatever Floats Your Boat
- [ ] RoVille

TYCOON

- [ ] Hospital Tycoon
- [ ] Clone Tycoon 2
- [ ] Tropical Resort Tycoon
- [ ] Mega Mansion Resort
- [ ] Mall Tycoon

SPORT

- [ ] Roblox Dodgeball
- [ ] Kick Off
- [ ] Sports City
- [ ] Phenom
- [ ] Super Striker League

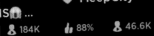

COUNTDOWN
Ninja Legends

👍 92% 👤 64.1K

Welcome to

Welcome to Bloxburg [BETA]

👍 95% 👤 33.8K

Royale High

👍 88% 👤 38.2K

🗡 **Jailbreak [CYBERTRUCK]**

👍 88% 👤 43.1K

Murder Mystery 2

👍 93% 👤 34.7K

[UPDATE] Tee Titans Battleg

👍 70% 👤 14.1

ated →

OBBY

- Wipeout Obby
- The Really Easy Obby
- Mega Fun Obby
- Escape the Bathroom Obby
- Escape Prison Obby

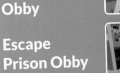

FIRST-PERSON SHOOTERS

- Zombie Uprising
- Energy Assault
- Shoot Out!
- Island Royale
- BIG Paintball!

ADVENTURE

- Robot 64
- Little World
- Hide and Seek Extreme
- SharkBite
- Royale High

SIMULATOR

- Laundry Simulator
- Animal Simulator
- Unboxing Simulator
- Bee Swarm Simulator
- Sonic Speed Simulator

FIGHTING

- Anime Fighters Simulator
- Ninja Legends
- Boss Fighting Simulator
- Muscle Legends
- Blox Fruits

STAYING SAFE, BEING SOCIAL

FOR PLAYERS

PICKING A USERNAME
NEVER choose a username that has your personal information, such as your real name or birthday.

STAY SECRET
Don't ever give out your real name, address, phone number, or the school you go to. Roblox will never need this info, and neither will anyone else. Roblox has chat software that will automatically try to filter out real-life names for a reason.

STAY IN-GAME
Scammers may ask you to trade money or items outside of the game. That's a good way to lose things. The trading menu in Roblox is designed to protect you, so stick to that and never give anything to people outside the game, no matter how trustworthy they may appear.

DON'T BE AFRAID TO REPORT
Players can easily mute and report inappropriate or abusive chat message, or disturbing content. Just use the Report Abuse system that's located on every single menu and Roblox will be notified and take action as soon as possible.

TELL YOUR PARENTS
Be brave. If someone is bothering you or you saw something you didn't like, tell a parent or guardian. Don't be afraid to say if someone is being inappropriate on Roblox. This game is for everyone and no one should be made to feel unsafe!

"I HEARD ABOUT A ROBUX GENERATOR!"
There are no such thing as Robux Generators – they're made up by scammers to steal money and accounts from players. Don't fall for it. Never trust any websites that aren't official. All official websites end with '.roblox.com'.

FOR PARENTS

BE INVOLVED
The best thing parents can do to make sure their children stay safe playing Roblox is to simply talk to them about the dangers. Make an account for yourself as you make one for your child. You'll even be able to add them as your child on Roblox, allowing you to ensure the social aspects of the game aren't getting in the way of them having fun.

"MY KID IS BEING BULLIED"
If someone is bothering your child, you should report and block them. By clicking on a username you can easily block a user and prevent them from ever contacting your child. By reporting abuse you can make sure that Roblox is aware of the situation.

SAFETY FEATURES
You can sign into your child's account and choose the level of privacy that they have. Make sure you choose the correct date of birth for your child as it sets the default security settings depending on how old they are. You can further modify the settings so that no one can contact your child, or that everyone can. Older players have more options.

MESSAGES AND CHAT
You can easily view your child's private message and chat histories from the main screen. You can also see your child's online friends, the games they've made, and anything they've purchased. If anything looks off, you can then take action.

PROTECTING YOUNGER CHILDREN
While Roblox is tamer than most games, some games feature violence or scary situations. You can go to the Account Restrictions section of your child's account to restrict them from playing anything too intense for their age group.

For many more resources we recommend going to Roblox's official parent's guide at: www.corp.roblox.com/parents There you'll find tutorials for navigating the platform, as well as tips for online safety.